My Body

Why do I brush my teeth?

Angela Royston

QED Publishing

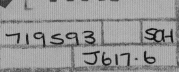
Copyright © QED Publishing 2009
First published in the UK in 2009 by
QED Publishing
A Quarto Group company
226 City Road
London ECIV 2TT

www.qed-publishing.co.uk

A catalogue record for this book is available
from the British Library.

ISBN 978 1 84835 214 8

Printed and bound in China.

Author Angela Royston
Consultant Terry Jennings
Project Editor Judith Millidge
Designer and Picture Researcher
     Louise Downey
Illustrator Chris Davidson

Publisher Steve Evans
Creative Director Zeta Davies
Managing Editor Amanda Askew

Words in **bold** are
explained in the glossary
on page 22.

Contents

Healthy teeth

Your teeth are very important. You need strong teeth to bite into your food and chew it so that it is easy to swallow. You have to brush your teeth regularly to keep them clean and strong.

You also use your teeth when you speak, especially your front teeth. For example, try to say the word 'teeth' without touching your front teeth with your tongue.

Your teeth help you to make 'hard' sounds like 't' and 'd'.

Activity

Use a mirror to check your teeth. How many do you have? Do you have any gaps?

5

Different shapes of teeth

You have three kinds of teeth. The front teeth have a wide, sharp edge, and are called incisors. You use them like a knife to slice through food.

Your front teeth are sharp and strong.

6

Behind your front teeth are four sharp canine teeth. You use your canine teeth to tear off mouthfuls of food.

The teeth at the back of your mouth are called molars. You use them for chewing.

Molar · Incisor · Canine ·

Teeth have different shapes so you can bite and chew food.

Activity

Put a piece of cracker between two spoons. Crush the cracker between the spoons. This is how your molars grind up food.

Two sets of teeth

You have two sets of teeth. The first set is called your baby teeth, or milk teeth. They begin to appear when you are about six to nine months old. By the time you are five, you will have 20 teeth.

Your first baby teeth usually appears in the bottom jaw.

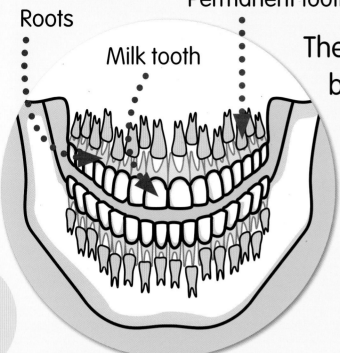

Roots

Permanent tooth

Milk tooth

Each milk tooth has a permanent tooth growing below it.

The second set of teeth grow below the milk teeth. They are called permanent or adult teeth, and there are 32 of them.

As each permanent tooth grows bigger, it pushes the milk tooth above it. This loosens the milk tooth until it falls out.

Activity

When a milk tooth falls out, examine it closely. Can you see any root? Compare its size to an adult tooth.

Inside a tooth

A tooth has three layers. The outer layer of **enamel** is the hardest thing in your body. The **dentine** below is as strong as bone. The centre is filled with soft **pulp** that contains blood vessels and nerves.

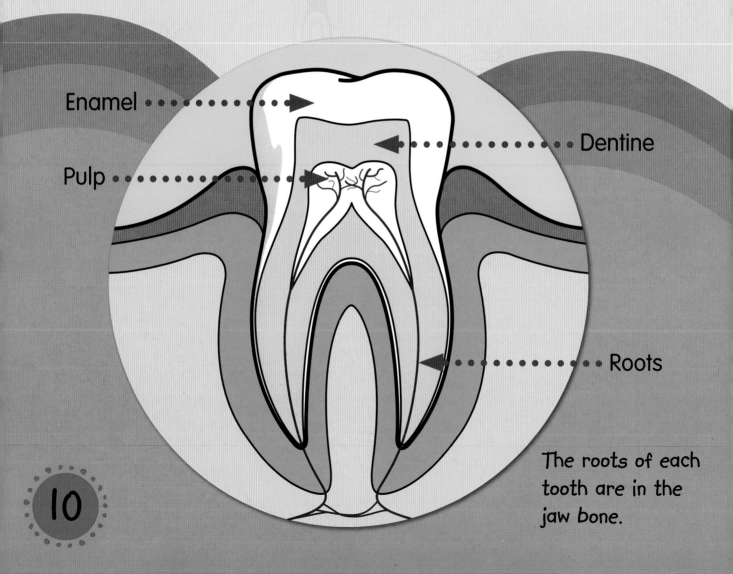

Enamel

Dentine

Pulp

Roots

The roots of each tooth are in the jaw bone.

Acid can damage your teeth by making a hole in the enamel. The hole is called **tooth decay**.

Activity

Put a whole uncooked egg in a glass, cover it with vinegar, and leave it overnight. Vinegar is an acid. It takes the **calcium** out of the eggshell in the same way that acid in your mouth attacks your teeth. In the morning, the eggshell will be soft.

11

What causes tooth decay?

Your mouth contains germs
called bacteria. They are too small to
see, but they feed on sugar left
in your mouth. As they feed,
they make **plaque**.

Plaque contains acid, which
can cause tooth decay.
Plaque and bacteria can also
affect your gums. They may
make your gums bleed.

When tooth decay causes a
hole or cavity, it can *be* very
painful. Children and adults can
suffer from tooth decay.

Dentists can treat tooth decay. They drill away the rotten part of the tooth and fill the hole. This is called a filling.

When a dentist fills a tooth, it stops decaying.

Activity

Find a large potato with one or more 'eyes' in it. With adult help, dig out the eyes with a potato peeler. Put a teaspoon of icing sugar into a bowl and add two drops of water. Use the mixture to fill the holes, like a dentist fills teeth.

13

Cleaning your teeth

Cleaning your teeth brushes away sugar and plaque. You should clean your teeth when you get up and before you go to bed. If possible, you should also clean them after meals.

Try to clean your teeth after eating anything sweet.

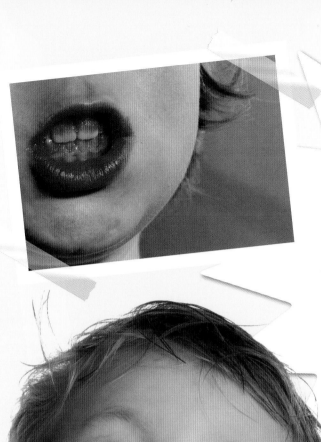

Activity

Disclosing tablets show how well you have brushed your teeth. When you suck one, it colours the plaque red or purple. Clean your teeth again until all the colour has gone.

Always brush from your gums to the tips of your teeth. Brush the back of each tooth as well as the front, and remember to clean the tops of your molars, as well as your gums.

Sugar damages your teeth

Fizzy drink

Doughnuts

Sweets

Sweet food and drinks are bad for your teeth. Fizzy drinks, cakes, biscuits, sweets and chocolate all contain lots of sugar. When you have swallowed them, some of the sugar stays in your mouth and can cause tooth decay.

Biscuits

Cake

These are just some of the foods and drinks that contain sugar.

16

Have a drink of water after eating or drinking something sweet. The water will help to wash the sugar away. Even better, clean your teeth.

Drinking water helps to clean your teeth.

Activity

Wash your toothbrush well in clean water after you have used it. Examine it carefully to make sure all the bits of food have been washed away.

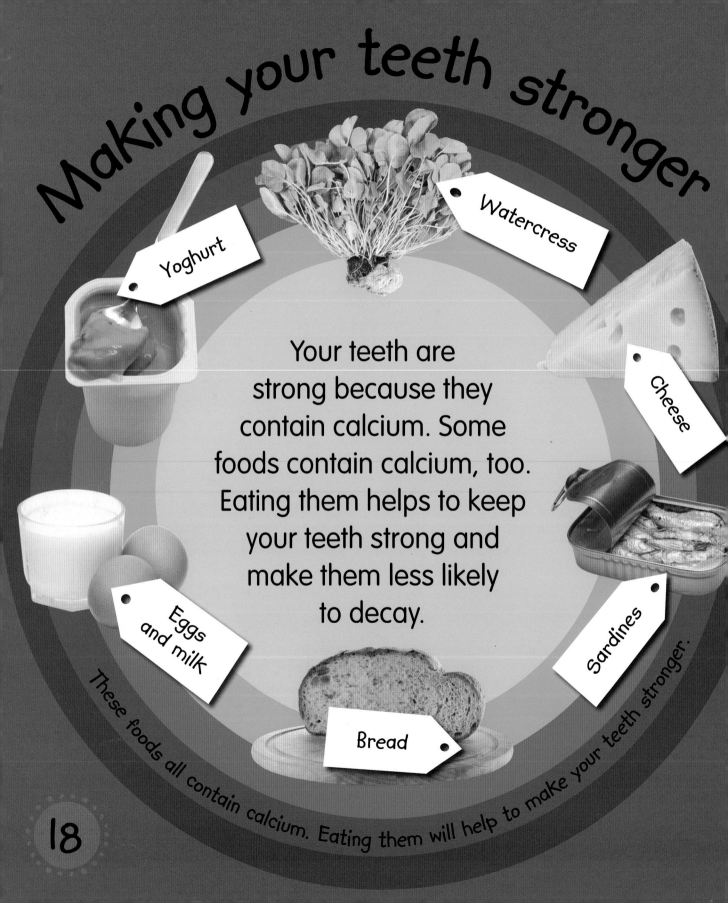

Making your teeth stronger

Watercress

Yoghurt

Cheese

Your teeth are strong because they contain calcium. Some foods contain calcium, too. Eating them helps to keep your teeth strong and make them less likely to decay.

Sardines

Eggs and milk

Bread

These foods all contain calcium. Eating them will help to make your teeth stronger.

18

Fluoride makes the enamel on your teeth stronger. Most types of toothpaste contain fluoride, and, in some places, fluoride is also added to tap water.

Try not to swallow the toothpaste. If you often have too much fluoride, it can discolour your teeth.

Activity

Make a healthy, calcium-filled lunch. You could start with a cheese, ham and salad sandwich. Then you could eat a yoghurt or an orange.

19

Going to the dentist

You should have a dental check-up every six months. The dentist looks at all your teeth to see if you have any tooth decay. The dentist also checks that your adult teeth are growing well.

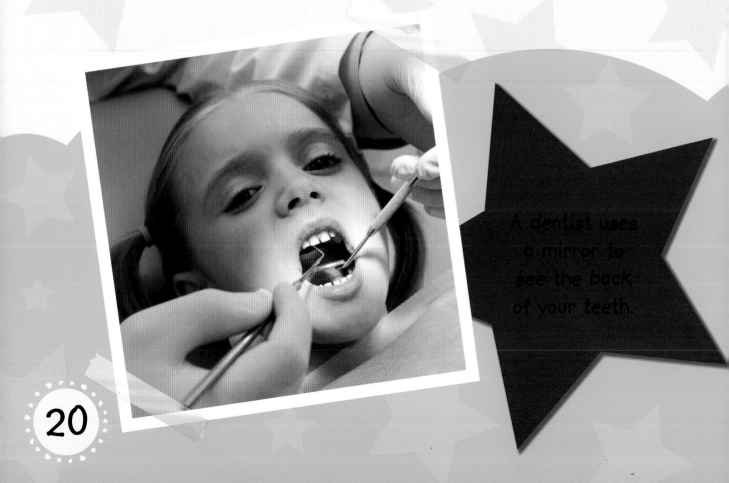

A dentist uses a mirror to see the back of your teeth.

You may sometimes get toothache in one of your teeth. It might be caused by eating something very cold. If you have toothache that does not go away, you should go to the dentist.

Cold food can make your teeth hurt, but just for a moment.

New

Old

Activity

Check your toothbrush to make sure the bristles are straight and firm. If they are not, you need a new toothbrush.

Glossary

Calcium
The substance that makes your teeth and bones hard and strong. Some foods also contain calcium, such as cheese and milk.

Dentine
The main part of a tooth is made of dentine. It is similar to bone and is covered with a layer of very hard enamel.

Enamel
The hard, glossy outer layer of a tooth. Enamel contains calcium and fluoride. It is the strongest substance in the body.

Fluoride
One of the substances that makes the enamel and dentine in your teeth strong. Most toothpastes contain fluoride.

Plaque
A sticky substance that is made by bacteria in your mouth. Plaque contains acid that can cause tooth decay. Cleaning your teeth helps to remove plaque and stop it forming.

Pulp
This is the soft material in the centre of a tooth. It includes blood vessels and nerves.

Tooth decay
A tooth decays when part of it rots. Tooth decay begins when acid in the mouth eats a hole in the enamel of a tooth. If it spreads to the soft pulp in the centre of the tooth, it can be very painful.

Notes for parents and teachers

1. Talk to the children about how cleaning their teeth helps to prevent tooth decay.

2. Search the Internet to find diagrams of a full set of milk teeth and a full set of permanent teeth. Count the teeth and see which extra teeth are included in the permanent teeth. Copy the plans of the teeth and help your child to colour in the milk teeth that they have already lost, and the permanent teeth that have already come through. Some families leave money from the 'Tooth Fairy' under a child's pillow whenever a milk tooth falls out.

3. Talk about tooth decay and the foods that contribute to it. Make a list of drinks and foods, particularly treats, that contain a lot of refined sugar. Discuss how you can limit the intake of these foods to once or twice a day, and how drinking water after having them or, better still, cleaning their teeth, helps to prevent tooth decay.

4. Encourage the children to suck a disclosing tablet after they have cleaned their teeth. Do the same yourself and compare how well you and the children have cleaned your teeth.

5. Take your child for a dental check up every six months. Set an example by having your own teeth checked at the same time.

Index